26

THEN AND THERE SERIES
GENERAL EDITOR
MARJORIE REEVES, M.A., Ph.D.

Wool Merchants of the Fifteenth Century

GLADYS SCOTT THOMSON

Illustrated from contemporary sources by

HAROLD BEARDS

LONGMANS

LONGMANS, GREEN AND CO LTD
48, Grosvenor Street, London W.1.
*Associated companies, branches and representatives
throughout the world*

First published 1958
Third impression 1964
Fourth impression 1966

Acknowledgments

For permission to include line drawings based on copyright sources we are indebted to the following: The Clarendon Press—page 2 from Price: *Portrait of Britain in the Middle Ages;* A. & C. Black, Ltd.—page 6 from Iris Brooke: *English Costume of the Later Middle Ages.*

Cover design by the girls of Lady Margaret School,
Parson's Green, S.W.6

Printed in Canada
by Evergreen Press Limited
Vancouver, B.C.

CONTENTS

TO THE READER

You all know how interesting letters can be when they tell us what the writer has been seeing and doing. The earliest letters in England were written in Latin and French. About the year 1400 a few people began to write their letters in English. Then more and more did so. After another 50 years nearly all private letters were written in English. Of course a great many of those letters were torn up or burnt or lost. But some were kept, which is very lucky for us. For if the Cely family, the wool-merchants, had not saved their letters, this little book could not have been written.

The Celys wrote these letters to one another five hundred years ago. In them they tell us all about their trade, how they bought and sold the wool. They also tell us about themselves, their horses and dogs and hawks; and how they bought gloves in France; and had a shooting match. So we can make a picture of their lives, real lives lived by the real people who were writing the letters, little thinking they would be read nearly five hundred years later. And because of what they tell us, we can go further and look at an old map of London and see where their house was. We can find pictures drawn in the days of the Celys which show us how they were dressed. We can see pictures of the ships in which they shipped their wool to France.

You will find many of the places mentioned in this book marked on the map on page 57. You will find the explanation of words printed like *this* in the Glossary on page 60. If there are any other words you do not know, look for their meanings in your dictionary.

THE CELY FAMILY

THIS is the story of a family who lived in London in the time of King Edward IV, almost exactly 500 years ago. Their name was Cely. The father was Richard Cely, and his wife was called Margaret. They had three sons, who were named Richard, Robert, and George.

In those days London was not the great town as we know it today. We should have thought it a very small place indeed. It stood on the north bank of the River Thames. At one end was the Tower of London. At the other end was a religious house called Black Friars: it was called Black Friars because the men who lived there were *friars*, who wore black gowns. Between these two the buildings stretched back as far as what we now call Holborn. That name means the bourne or little river in the Hole or valley. The river ran on through London to the Thames. Further down it was called the Fleet. We know today the street called Fleet Street. In the time of the Celys there was no Fleet Street, only the river. But there were many other streets, narrow to our way of thinking, and *cobbled*. There were some fine houses in some of them and many churches.

Nearly all round the town was the Wall of London as it had been built by the Romans and later repaired or partially rebuilt. But in some places this wall was already

I

beginning to break down a little. Already, too, houses and buildings were beginning to appear outside the wall. London was growing fast. Here is a map of London about the time of the Celys:

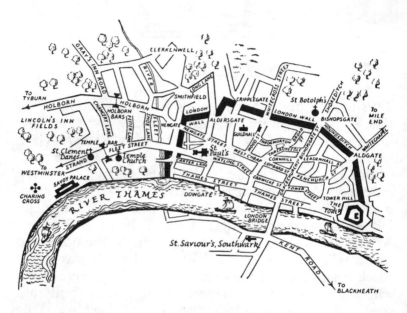

Although London was still a small town to our way of thinking, it was a very important one. Its citizens, among whom were the Cely family, were very proud of their city. A poet at this time calls London "the flower of cities all". He says:

> Strong be the wall that about thee stands,
> Wise be the people that within thee dwells,
> Fresh be thy river with its lusty *strands*,
> Blithe be thy churches, well sounding thy bells,
> Rich be thy merchants in *substance* that excels.

Among those merchants were the Celys. If they were not perhaps very rich, they were at least very comfortably off. Their house was in the street still called Mark Lane. This street was at the end where the Tower of London stood. It ran down towards the River Thames. We shall read soon how convenient it was for the Celys to be near the river. There were two churches close by. One was called All Hallows. The other was St. Olave's. The Cely family probably attended the church of St. Olave's. They must often have heard the bells of both churches and perhaps of others also as the poem says. Here is a sketch of London churches made by someone living rather before the Celys' time:

The Cely house was half-way down Mark Lane. We know a little of what it must have looked like.

Facing the street there was a gateway, through which those going to the Cely house must pass. This gateway was built up over the top, with a small building or house there containing two rooms. If you know an old gateway, perhaps it too has a building on the top and you will know that there are one or even two small rooms inside. Going through the gateway we should find ourselves in a courtyard. Probably there were buildings on both sides of this courtyard. Some of them were storerooms. We shall see presently what they were used for. But it is quite likely that the kitchen and some larders were there also; they were often quite separate from the house.

Opposite the gateway was the house itself. The door opened into the courtyard. Going through the door we should have found ourselves in what was generally called the Great Parlour. We should think it more like a hall. In this parlour the family lived and ate. There would have been one long table or perhaps even two tables. They were mounted on trestles so that they could easily be taken down and put away. There were benches on which the family sat to eat their meals. There were also stools on which they could sit round the fire which blazed on the hearth. The fire was made of logs, for there was very little coal at this time. There might have been just one chair— which was kept for the master of the house, old Richard Cely. As we know the Celys were well-to-do, they certainly had a sort of sideboard on which would be probably some silver bowls or silver-and-wood bowls. They had knives and spoons for their meals but no forks; it would be a long time still before forks would come into use at meals.

4

Here is what the Great Parlour looked like:

Probably there was another little parlour at the back of the Great Parlour, and there were certainly one or two bedrooms on the ground floor. Upstairs there were more bedrooms. The chief bedroom had a great bed like a four-poster. This would most likely be for Richard and his wife Margaret. The other rooms would have had some narrow beds. There were no chairs. All the rooms, or nearly all, would have had cupboards into which to put clothes.

5

This picture shows the clothes which Richard Cely and his son would wear.

Richard Cely the elder is wearing a long plain gown, belted at the waist. From the belt hangs a bag which was used as a purse. His sons probably had these gowns also, and when they went out, they wore round *stuff* caps with the gowns. But if the young men wanted to look smart they dressed like young Richard in this picture. He is wearing long close-fitting tights, that is stockings and breeches made in one, and over these a short tunic with full sleeves. When he put on his tights and tunic, he probably wore a peaked cap instead of the ordinary round stuff one. All of them had very full cloaks to wrap round them. These cloaks were made of a coarse heavy woollen material that kept out the rain nearly as well as a macintosh does. The shoes for outdoors were of leather. Those to

6

wear in the house were often of woollen material. Rich grand folk wore velvet shoes. The Celys probably wore shoes made of wool or leather. You can see here what sort of clothes the women of the Cely family wore.

Their house was of course the place where they lived, their home. But it was more than this, for it was their place of business also. This was nearly always so 500 years ago. Men did not live in one place and go out to business every day to another. They carried on their business in their own houses. We have seen that the Celys were merchants of London. Their business was buying wool and selling it again. Let us see what this wool trade was. Then we can find out from their own letters the part this family of father and sons played in it.

7

THE WOOL TRADE

In the House of Lords at Westminster you can see a seat which looks like a large square bag. It is stuffed with wool. It has no back or arms and is covered with cloth. This is called the Woolsack. This is the seat of the *Lord Chancellor*. If you look at a picture of the House of Lords 500 years ago you will see that the Woolsack was there then too, and here is a Lord Chancellor who lived about the time of the Celys sitting on it with his two clerks:

The Woolsack reminds us how important the wool trade was for England. Here is the reason. Wool was wanted to make the cloth that everyone—men, women and children —needed for their clothes, everywhere. A great deal of

8

this cloth was made abroad. One country in particular, Flanders, was celebrated for its cloth. But the *Flemish* weavers needed good wool to make good cloth. And they knew that the best wool was that grown on English sheep. Therefore they were ready to buy wool from England and to give good prices for it. This brought much money into England. It was men like the Cely family who arranged for the selling of the wool to the weavers. But first they had to buy it from the farmers who kept the sheep.

The Sheep Farms

As wool was so much wanted, there were many sheep-farmers and sheep-farms. We know a good deal about them, just because wool was such an important trade. There are many pictures of the sheep and what happened to their wool throughout the year. People wrote about the sheep and their wool. Also the farmers had to keep accounts, so that they would know how much their sheep cost them and how much money they got from the sale of the wool.

There were sheep-farms in many different places in England. The one thing necessary was that the grass should be good enough for the sheep to feed on. But of course in some parts of England it was much better than others, so that the sheep that grazed there grew better wool. One such district was the hilly country in Gloucestershire called the Cotswolds. As we shall see when we read their letters, it was to the Cotswolds that the Celys generally went to buy the wool they were going to sell to the Flemish weavers.

Some Cotswold wool farmers became very rich, and built beautiful stone houses. You can still see this house, built in Chipping Campden by William Greville, an important wool merchant:

Some farmers had only a few sheep, which they looked after themselves. Perhaps the wife or a son or daughter would help. But other farmers had a great number of sheep, with shepherds to look after them. These shepherds were really very important. There was a great deal written about them. One writer says that they must be watchful, and take care nothing happened to the sheep they were looking after. He says they must treat the sheep kindly, so that the sheep would trust them and keep by them and not get scattered. The shepherds generally had a dog to help them; this writer recommended a dog with a good bark. Here is a shepherd playing his pipe while his flock grazes peacefully and his dog keeps watch:

Besides their wages the shepherds were given presents. The master in most places gave them one of the lambs when the *ewes* were having their lambs. They also got one *fleece* of wool for themselves when the sheep were *sheared*. If they had a sheep or two of their own they were allowed to keep them with their master's sheep on his *pasture*. But they also had a very busy and in some ways a hard life for much of the year. There was a great deal for them to do, as well as for the farmer and his family. Here are some more shepherds tending their flocks:

The Sheep-Farmer's Year

In the Cotswolds the beginning of the season on the sheep farms was January and February. Then the lambs were being born. This was an anxious time for the farmer, because his profits for the year depended on how many lambs were born, and how many of them were strong and would grow up into sheep with good wool. We know that he and his helpers, whether his family or his shepherds, would often have to sit up all night. Generally they sat in one of the sheds near the sheep-folds. The folds were enclosures built of stone in which sheep were kept during the cold months. The farmer would lay in a good stock of candles to help see in the darkness. Probably his wife made the candles herself at home from tallow.

Sometimes heavy snow fell at lambing time. That made the farmer more anxious. He and his shepherds would wade through the snow to find the baby lambs and their mothers. Then the lambs would be brought into a warm place, perhaps a shed or even the kitchen of the house. If a lamb were very weak or if its mother had died it would be fed with milk brought from the dairy. We can see from accounts kept by the farmers how many lambs were born, how many died, how many lost their mothers, and how many were strong and well.

After this a rather important time was when the dairymaids were able to take milk from the ewes who had had lambs. They used it to make cheeses. Have you ever tried a cheese made from ewes' milk? It is very good! A great many cheeses were made in those days on the sheep-farms.

Here are the dairymaids milking the ewes:

But the really great day was when the time came to shear the sheep for their wool. This was usually some time in May. Where a farmer had many sheep it was a big business. First all the different flocks had to be collected and driven to the place where there were the sheds for the shearing. We can make a picture of the farmer and his helpers with their *crooks* driving the sheep from the different fields, with the dog, or perhaps more than one dog, barking and running round the sheep to get them into their proper places. But before the sheep were got into the sheds something else had to be done to them. They had to be washed. For this reason the shearing sheds were always if possible near water, perhaps by a stream or brook, perhaps by a pond. A poet, Thomas Tusser, who knew all about country life, wrote:

Wash sheep for the better where water does run
And let him go cleanly and dry in the sun.

Of course this washing was very necessary. We can be sure that when merchants like the Celys came to buy the wool they would inspect it very closely to see if it were in good condition. Nobody wanted to buy dirty wool, or, as sometimes happened, wool that had got earth or even thorns and leaves mixed in with it after the sheep had been lying down or rubbing themselves in the hedges.

Once the washing was over there came the great day or days of the shearing. First the wool was cut from the backs of the sheep. This had to be very carefully done. As a rule neither the farmer nor the shepherds undertook this. Special people who understood how to cut off the wool were engaged. They were called clippers, because they clipped the wool. They were not always men; very often a clipper was a woman.

14

But the clippers in this picture are men. You can
see how carefully they have to hold the sheep so that it
cannot struggle free or be cut by the sharp shears.

When the wool had been cut by the clippers it was
wound on cards. These were like the cards used today to
wind wool or cotton on. But the cards used for winding
the wool then were very much bigger than any used now.
We can be sure that the owner of the sheep watched very
carefully the shearing and the clipping and then the winding of the wool. He knew that he could not sell the wool
unless it was properly prepared and carefully wound.

At last all was done. The sheep had been washed and the
wool cut from their backs and they had been sent out to
graze again, looking rather naked. Their wool had been all
combed out and carded and was all ready for the buyers.

Each grower marked his sacks with special marks like these:

Then came the great day of holiday. There was a feast for everyone who had taken part in the work. Afterwards there was music and dancing. Although William Shakespeare lived a hundred years after the Celys, he knew all about these feasts. Very likely he had watched one as a boy when he lived at Stratford-on-Avon in Warwickshire. He may even have taken part in one. He certainly wrote a very good description of such a feast in his play which he calls 'The Winter's Tale'. We can be fairly sure that his feast was very much the same as those of a hundred years earlier, for in the country and on the sheep-farms there had been very little change.

Shakespeare first shows the farmer and his people getting ready for the feast. All farms had pigs and geese and chickens. There would certainly have been roast pork and roast goose to eat as well as chickens. But the chickens were generally boiled; in those days people seem to have preferred their chickens boiled and not roasted. There would have been plenty of eggs and milk and butter on the farm. The farmer's wife would have made many loaves of bread. But she would also have made pies and a number of sweet dishes, some of them tarts, some of them more like our custards. In order to make these things, the farmer's wife would send someone away to the nearest town to buy certain things for her. Shakespeare tells of the orders given to the man who was to fetch the goods. He has the list in his hands, and says, "Let me see, what am I to buy for our sheep shearing feast?" He was to bring back three pounds of sugar; five pounds of currants; rice; saffron, which was a yellow plant used to colour the pastries and cakes; nutmegs and ginger; four pounds of prunes and four pounds of raisins. They called these last "raisins of the sun" because the grapes from which they were made had been spread out in the sun to dry.

We can imagine how gay everyone was when they came to sit at the well-spread tables. There would be a piper there who played on his *pipe* while they ate. Nearly all pictures having anything to do with sheep and shepherds show that when there was playing and music it was nearly always a pipe that was used. The scene would look all the gayer because every person, according to custom, had his or her *nosegay* of flowers. In the feast in 'The Winter's Tale' the farmer's wife had made up as many as twenty-four nosegays. The month was May or early June, so there were plenty of flowers to be had. Shakespeare's shepherdess says that the fairest flowers of the season are the carnations. She also talks about marigolds and sweet-smelling lavender. We know, too, that there were always wallflowers; they were called gilly-flowers and were great favourites. The nosegays must have looked very pretty and smelt very sweetly.

After the feast came dancing to the pipes, and singing as well. One song in 'The Winter's Tale' goes like this:

> Jog on, jog on the footpath way,
> And merrily hent the stile-a:
> A merry heart goes all the day,
> Your sad tires in a mile-a.

Here are some merry-makers dancing to the music of some sort of stringed instrument:

There was another collecting of wool later in the year. But this was rather different. About October the farmer had to kill many of his sheep. This was because in those days no one knew how to feed sheep through the winter on roots like swedes or turnips. So, because there was only enough grass in winter-time for just a few sheep, the others had to be killed. But their wool was not wasted. The whole fleece was cut from their backs and sold like that.

We can imagine how anxiously the farmer would look out for buyers who would buy and pay for his wool after the first sheep-shearing and then again after the fleeces had been cut. There was a saying at the time: "It is the sheep that pay for all".

18

Buying the Wool

Among the men who came to buy the wool were the Cely family. The father, Richard, was growing old. He did not often go after the wool himself but left that part to his sons. It was mostly the eldest son, also Richard, who generally went to the Cotswolds.

We can see from his letters how he would set out on his horse from their London house. The first part of the road near London would be fairly good. Farther from London the road was no more than a rough track, along which a horse could go only very slowly, sometimes stumbling. But there were often grassy paths along the side. We can be sure that Richard Cely, like other travellers, turned his horse to ride along them whenever possible. It made the riding easier for him, and it was much easier for the horse. Here is a traveller who may have met Richard on his journey:

The Celys were very fond of horses. They often speak about them in their letters and give their names. Richard writes to his brother:

> This same day I depart into Cotswold . . . and there rides with me William, upon Pye your horse; and I have with me my *falconer* . . .

The falconer was the man who looked after the falcons or hawks who sat on their wrists or their master's wrists and were trained to fly after such birds as *herons* or partridges and bring them back to their master. So we know Richard Cely often enjoyed some sport on his two or three days' journey. Here is a gay hawking party:

But hawking was only an amusement. Richard's real business was serious. When he reached the places in the Cotswolds where he meant to buy the wool, he had to examine it carefully and see that it was good value for his money.

The principal farmer from whom George bought wool was named William Midwinter, who lived at North Leach.

The Cotswold wool was dear, but it was probably very good. Richard generally bought a great amount. He and the farmer would pack it into great sacks. Then horses carried the sacks to London.

Sometimes Richard had adventures of his own. He was not married and he was considered a very good match. So, many people were anxious for him to marry one of their daughters. Once when he had been three weeks in the Cotswolds buying wool, William Midwinter suggested there was a young lady in whom he might be interested and that he should wait to see her. Richard writes:

> I said I would tarry ... and the same day came the young gentlewoman and her stepmother. I and William Brettin were saying *matins* when they came into church. When matins were done they went to a *kinswoman* of the young gentlewoman. I sent them a *pottle* of white wine and they took it thankfully for they had come a mile on foot that morning. When my work was done I came and welcomed them and kissed them and they thanked me for the wine and prayed me come to dinner with them. I excused myself and they made me promise to drink with them after dinner. I sent them for dinner a gallon of wine. They sent me a roast heron. After dinner I came and drank with them ... We had right good communication and the person pleases me well ...

Roast heron seems strange to us. But in those days people were very fond of eating both herons and swans. They were generally roasted, and stuffed in the way we stuff a goose. When a swan was served on a great occasion, as at the King's table, it was very elaborately decorated with feathers. Probably the heron sent to Richard was

21

just a plain roast bird. We must hope that he enjoyed it before he went round to drink wine with his friends. But though he liked his companions and found the young lady quite attractive, sad to say he rode away the next day and never came back to see her again.

In the meantime he had despatched the wool he had bought to London. The great sacks were piled on both sides of the horses used for the purpose. They had to be strong horses because they had the heavy loads to carry over rough roads. Because they carried packs of all kinds, not only wool, they are often called *pack-horses*. Can you see the pack on this horse?

As the horses and the men with them neared London, they crossed the bridge over the Thames and turned and came up Mark Lane to the Cely house. The sacks were taken from the horses' backs and carried into the court-yard. Then they were put into one of the storerooms at the side. So we see now the use of these storerooms. We can be sure that old Richard Cely, the father, was on the lookout for the arrival of the wool, and that he would come into the storeroom to see the sacks opened. It is certain that when this was done he put his hand in and pulled out some of the wool and examined it closely to see if his son had bought well. After all, the wool was not going to stay there in the storeroom. It had been bought from the Gloucestershire sheep-farms, and now it was going to be sold again. Old Richard Cely hoped to get a good price for it.

Where the Wool was Sold

So the next business was to sell the wool. We may be surprised to learn that it was not sold in England. But we have already heard that English wool was much in demand by weavers on the Continent for making cloth. They were eager to get it. They were ready to pay very good prices for it. Therefore it was best to take the wool across the English Channel to some place to which foreign buyers could easily come. It was a very good thing for English traders that a town on the other side of the Channel actually belonged to England and had been made a great place to which English goods could be sent and sold.

This town was Calais. Today, as we all know, Calais is a French town, but in the time of the Celys it belonged to the English. Let us look back earlier in history for a little. We shall find out how Calais came to be an English town. We shall also learn how it was that the Celys, like many other merchants, knew Calais well and did so much business there. We shall have to go back to the war called the Hundred Years War and the days of King Edward III.

23

HOW CALAIS CAME TO BE AN ENGLISH TOWN

England and France were at war with each other for a hundred years off and on. There were intervals of peace. But war always broke out again. We remember that during that war the soldiers of Edward III won a battle near a village called Crécy. Crécy was on the River Somme near the English Channel.

After the victory at Crécy, Edward's soldiers marched northwards. There on the coast was the town called Calais. It was a small town but very important. It was a port, and so was very strongly fortified. Edward's army found they could not break down the fortifications and get into the town, so they settled down in their tents outside the walls. There was a siege. The inhabitants of Calais could not get out of the town and no one could get in to them. That meant that no food could get in either. There was still the harbour, but Edward sent his ships to stay outside the harbour entrance, so the way in by water was also blocked, and nothing could get in that way. The men and women of Calais held out for more than a year, but every month there was less food to eat, and at last they were starving. Then they had to give in. The French soldiers marched out from the fortifications with their swords reversed. This meant they surrendered to the English. The gates were opened and the English soldiers marched in.

Here is a picture of a town with a besieging army all round it:

At that time King Edward III had come over to be with his army and he had with him his Queen, Philippa. It was August 1347. Perhaps you have heard the story of how the King sat in the hall of the burghers with the Queen beside him. Everyone in Calais was afraid that the English soldiers would be allowed to kill the men and women of the town and take their goods. Six of the leading men came to see the King. They wore only shirts and they had put rope halters round their necks. They told Edward he might hang them then and there if only he would spare the town and the rest of the people living there. Philippa was so sorry for the town and thought these men so brave that she threw herself before her husband and begged him not to hang them and not to let the rest of the inhabitants suffer. Edward granted her request and said she could do what she liked with the six men. We know that she was very kind to them. She had clothes found for them and she gave them food. The English soldiers were not allowed to kill the other men and women. But in one way Calais did suffer.

The leading merchants were told they must leave the town and give up their businesses to merchants who would come from England. Only about twenty French merchants were allowed to remain. The place of the others was taken by men who came over from England.

So you can see how the Celys and other English traders came to be in business in Calais 100 years later. For 200 years after its surrender, until the reign of Queen Mary Tudor, Calais remained an English town with an English garrison of soldiers and many English inhabitants. The town was of great importance to England. It was only 33 miles across the Channel to Dover. It had a good harbour and could have good fortifications built round it, as the soldiers of Edward III had discovered. If and when England was at war with France and wanted to invade that country, Calais was an open door through which the soldiers could pass. But there was another reason which made it more important still. It could be a centre for English trade on the Continent. That is why the French merchants were made to leave the town and English merchants were sent there.

Soon the King issued a proclamation which made Calais what was known as a *Staple* town, that is to say that goods for export must be sent to Calais and sold there by merchants appointed for the purpose. Other people could not sell. Of course there were other Staple towns abroad, and in England as well. But Calais was so important that it was often called 'The Staple'. One can imagine that merchants in England who had goods they wanted to sell abroad would be anxious to be given the right to do so in Calais. When they were given that right they were called Merchants of the Staple. The Celys, father and sons, had that right, and letters to them were often addressed thus:

> The Right Worshipful Masters
> Richard and George Cely,
> Merchants of the Staple of
> Calais.

They had the right, too, to use this special staplers' mark:

We know that what the Celys wanted to sell was the wool they had bought from the farmers in the Cotswolds. And here Calais had a great advantage, which explains why it was the chief place for the sale of wool. If you look at a map you will see that Calais was not far from the border of the country known then as Flanders, part of the Netherlands or Low Countries. (Today we know part of Flanders by the name of Belgium.) It stretched from just beyond Calais right up to the great estuary of the River Scheldt. Among its important towns were Bruges and Ghent and Ypres. It had a great industry. The Flemish workmen were famous for their skill in weaving wool into cloth. But before these weavers could get to work they had to get the wool. Now we can see why Calais, quite close to Flanders, was such a splendid centre for the English merchants who wanted to sell the wool. And we remember, too, that the English wool was good wool and therefore the Flemish merchants were most anxious to buy it for their weavers.

If then the wool was to be sold in Calais, someone had to be there to do the selling. The Celys had their house and place of business in London in Mark Lane. But one son, George, was sent to live in Calais among other English merchants there. He was the one who had to do the selling. Of course, George would sometimes come over to England and his brother Richard would cross to Calais. The father never did; perhaps he thought he was too old for the sea voyage. But although the brothers Richard and George did go to and fro, it was Richard and his father who were responsible for all the business in Mark Lane, while George was responsible for business in Calais. This meant that a great many letters had to be written. It is from those letters, which have fortunately been kept, that we know so much about the Cely family and their wool business.

Also in the business was someone called William Cely. He was not a son of old Richard. He was a relative taken into the trade, perhaps a nephew. He was not himself a Merchant of the Staple, but he was evidently a most useful person, travelling to and fro between London and Calais, and undertaking a great deal of work. We have some of his letters also.

GETTING READY FOR THE JOURNEY

To get the wool from the house in Mark Lane to George Cely in Calais took a great deal of time and preparation. The first business was to pack the wool. This was done by putting it in *canvas*, which was then sewn up. The packets made were called *sarplers*, and generally two bags of wool were put in each sarpler. Both canvas and the thread for sewing it had to be very strong. Much better canvas was made in the Flemish towns than could be got in England, and the pack thread made at Calais was particularly good. So we find old Richard Cely writing to George that he is to buy Flemish canvas and "three dozen pack thread" at Calais for the packing of the wool in London.

This packing up into sarplers was only the beginning of the business. The Celys could not just take the packets and send them off. They had first to be taken to the Customs House. If you look at an old map of London, you will notice that all along the banks of the Thames between the Tower of London and London Bridge there were wharfs and quays. Just about in the middle was the Customs House, which perhaps looked like this:

29

Now we can see how convenient it was for the Celys to live in Mark Lane. They were quite near the river and not far from the Customs House. The sarplers were taken to the Customs House by the Celys' men, carrying them or pushing them on a cart. Can you see three ways of carrying wool to the Customs House in the picture? (Do you think that the man in the middle is going to enjoy chicken for his supper?)

Either Richard Cely, the son, or perhaps William Cely went too. For there was money to be paid out. All merchants had to pay for being allowed to send their wool away to be sold. First of all each sarpler was weighed. To show this had been done, a seal, called the Seal of the Staple, was put on each sack. After this the Customs officials wrote all the particulars in a book. Then they told Richard Cely or anyone who came instead of him what he had to pay. After that he was given a paper called a *cocket*. On this paper was written how much all his sarplers of wool weighed and exactly how much he had paid the Customs.

Then at last the Celys' men could pick up the sacks again and carry them to the quay on the riverside, where they were to be loaded on to ships. We can see from the picture what a busy river the Thames was; do you see the houses *on* London Bridge?

There was always coming and going on the quays, as there was on the river. We can imagine that with passengers and men carrying goods everywhere, there would be a great deal of tramping about, mud in wet weather, and all kinds of rubbish would be dropped. The Corporation of London made very strict rules about this. They wanted to keep the approaches to the river clean. Of course, it was important to the merchants who brought in or took out goods for sale that their goods should not get dirty. So the men who had the ships were made to pay for the

31

cleaning. The order said that 12*d*. or 8*d*. was to be collected from each ship or boat for "cleaning and keeping clean the ports, quays, etc., where such boats discharge". Perhaps we are not surprised to learn that the rule was not as well kept as it might be. But we must hope that that quay was nice and clean and that it was not raining when the Celys' sarplers of wool were carried down to it from the Customs House.

Here the sarplers are being loaded into a small boat which will carry them out to the fine ship that is ready to leave. You can see the ship's crew setting the sails to catch the stiff breeze that will blow them to Calais.

SETTING SAIL

The Cely family had a boat of their own, called MARGARET CELY after the mother of the family. We shall hear something about this ship presently. But the Celys did not always send their wool in it. Like other merchants, they also used ships whose business it was to go to and from English to French and other ports, carrying goods and passengers, for which the master of the ship was paid.

Generally the sarplers were divided among several ships. These ships were very small indeed compared with those we know today. One ship could not carry nearly all the sarplers that merchants like the Celys sent out. Also it was better to divide the loads for safety. Then, if one ship was lost, at least it could be hoped the others would get safely to Calais with their load of wool. So on one day we hear of the Celys' sarplers being put on to no fewer than six different ships waiting at the quay. We know their names. They were MARY of London, CHRISTOPHER of Rainham, THOMAS of Maidstone, MARY GRACE of London, MICHAEL of Hull, and THOMAS of Newhithe. We notice that only two of these were London ships. Others belonged to other ports round the coast; much wool was sent out from these other ports as well as from London, but the ships from these ports would often come up the Thames for a London cargo too.

When the sarplers were on board, there was a wait for the arrival of an official called a 'searcher'. His business

33

was to see that the number of sarplers put on the ship was exactly the same as was written down on the cocket. So we have one reason why it was important for this paper to be kept. The Celys, like other merchants, had to show they had not smuggled a few extra sarplers on board without going through the Customs House and paying for them.

We know on which ship the packs or sarplers had been loaded when the searchers came to look at them. There were 7½ in the CHRISTOPHER of Rainham; 7 in the MARY of London; 6 each in the THOMAS of Maidstone and the MARY GRACE of London. In the MICHAEL of Hull there was only 1 pack. In the THOMAS of Newhithe there was also 1 pack with a few *fells*, pieces tied together in a bundle. We can imagine that the MICHAEL and the THOMAS were very small ships indeed. We can see from drawings what they looked like. Mostly they had a deck, and a mast for the sail, and sometimes a second mast, a small one at the stern of the ship. Once the sarplers of wool were in, there was not much room for the crew.

But the ships had quite a number of sailors. We know this from the MARGARET CELY, a ship with a deck and two masts. She had a crew of 19 men. The important men were the Captain, for he was called Master, the boatswain and the cook. The boatswain had to look after the sails and the rigging, and it was his duty to call the crew to their work with a whistle. Perhaps you have heard of a bosun's whistle? We may be surprised a cook was necessary on such a short voyage. But, as we shall see, the voyage to Calais might take several days or the ship might be going farther, perhaps to Bordeaux. In fact, one of the duties of the searcher after he had looked at the sarplers of wool, was to find out whether there was a proper store of

34

provisions. We know what these provisions would have been from the account books kept for the MARGARET CELY. She was *victualled* with beef and fish, some of each already salted, wheat and beer. Here are some prices from the account books of the man who did the buying for the MARGARET CELY.

item.	paid for a barrel of beer for the ship.	8*d.*
item.	paid for bread at Sandwich for the ship.	8*d.*
item.	paid to Tounshead the baker for bread for the MARGARET.	10*s.* 6*d.*
item.	3 *quarterns* of wheat.	20*s.*
item.	for a barrel of beef.	13*s.* 4*d.*
item.	for an ox.	15*s.* 4*d.*
item.	paid for a salt fish for the ship.	4*d.*
item.	for a quarter and a half of fish.	20*s.*
item.	for a *peck* of salt.	6*d.*
item.	for 2 *bushels* of salt.	2*s.*

The beef in the barrel would have been in salt, and some of the fish was already salted. If they were bought fresh they were put into salt on the ship. That is why so much salt was always bought. There seems to have been quite a lot of bread bought. But the sailors were hungry folk. The wheat was for the cook to make more bread when the rest had been eaten up.

Other things had to be laid in besides food. After all, the ships were on the river or on the sea by night as well as day. Some kind of light had to be provided. So in the account book there is often an entry

item.	for 2 dozen candles.	3*s.* 9*d.*

Can you imagine sailing along on a dark night with the ship lit only by a few flickering candles?

35

Now the ships have got the wool stowed away and the provisions on board. The searcher has looked at both and it is time for him to take his fee and be off. But he does not always go. He will have to give up the fee at the Customs House. What he wants is a tip to buy himself a drink, and sometimes he hangs about until he gets it. Of course the merchants had to keep the searcher in a good temper, otherwise he might turn nasty and complain about the sarplers, or say there were not enough provisions on board, and so delay the sailing of the ship. But at last he has gone. Then once the tide was high, the ships, with their precious cargo, put off from the quayside and sailed away to Calais.

THE VOYAGE

We can think of the ships with their sails set passing down the River Thames, seeing other ships and little rowing-boats on their way. Then they reached the mouth of the river and so came to the open sea. We can imagine an anxious watch was kept on the weather. If the right wind was blowing, all would be well for the sailing-vessels. But there might be no wind at all. Then they would be becalmed and have to lie at anchor. Or there might be a fog. Or there might be too much wind blowing in the wrong direction so that the small vessels would be blown out of their way. If the wind became a gale the waves would break over them and perhaps wreck them.

The ship in the picture below probably struck a rock near the coast—but we do not know that it was carrying any of the Cely wool.

So we can see that the time taken to get the wool to France would be very uncertain. It might be done, if the wind was very favourable, in twenty-four hours. It might take several days—or it might never arrive at all. Now we see how important the provisions were.

The ships, too, usually carried barrels of tar and pitch. They were used for plastering on the places where the ship's planks were joined together, so making them water-tight. In an emergency the barrels of tar could be set alight as a distress signal. There were other dangers besides bad weather. Even if there was a fair wind and no fog and no gale, the sailors might still get into trouble. They might be attacked. This often happened when England and France were so continually at war. French ships would follow the English vessels and try to seize them. The English ships did the same to the Frenchmen.

Even in peace-time there were always pirates in the Channel. You have perhaps read stories about pirates—sea-robbers. They put out to sea to look for ships carrying goods, then they fought them and, if they could, robbed them of their goods. There were plenty of these pirates about, English as well as French. They were not at all particular whom they attacked as long as they could get the goods. The crews in the ships that carried the Celys' wool knew all about watching for the sea-robbers and being ready to fight them back if they tried to get the sarplers of wool from them.

If we think of the war and the pirates we are not surprised to find that all or nearly all the ships that went to sea were armed. We know something about the arms that were bought for the MARGARET CELY. She had cannon, and bows and arrows, and darts that could be

38

thrown at a pirate ship. The account books show some of the things that were bought.

item.	For gun-powder.	4s. 8d.
item.	a dozen bow strings.	5d.
item.	a quart of *resin*.	11d.

The gunpowder was for the cannon, and the resin was to rub on the bow strings to prevent them from breaking. In this sea-fight two men are hitting at each other with planks!

Some of the letters sent to the Celys in Mark Lane tell tales of some fights, though not with their own ship. In February 1484 they told how on one Thursday "a ship came out of Dover Harbour to go to Calais" and "she was chased by Frenchmen and driven into Dunkirk Harbour". In March a pirate ship, English this time, was in the Channel. The letter tells how

Richard Awray set forth for warfare in a ship of his own— and as he came to Calais two French men-of-war met him and fought with him and there he was slain and several of his company. They say 8 or 9 persons in all, on whose souls Jesu have mercy.

So what with gales and rough seas and trouble from pirates we can see how perilous was the passage to Calais. It is no wonder that when letters were written by anyone starting on a voyage there would be added a prayer such as "Holy Trinity speed us".

As the small ships sailed into Calais harbour, those on board would look at the town. It was a walled town. That wall was very necessary because, as we have heard, Calais could be attacked from the sea as well as from the land. Guns could be mounted on the wall, and at intervals all along it there were towers from which other guns could be fired or archers could shoot arrows.

Behind the walls were the houses and the streets, the churches and the Guildhall, which had been built for the Staplers. This picture shows what a sailor would see as he sailed into the harbour at Calais:

In front of the wall were the quays for the ships. When the MARGARET CELY or one of the other boats in which the family were interested came into the harbour she would tie up at one of these quays. We can be sure they were very carefully watched. The men in the towers on the wall were there in times of peace as well as of war. One of their duties was to keep a very sharp lookout on every boat they saw on the sea. We have heard already in the Cely letters how pirate ships would lie in the Channel waiting to attack the boats carrying wool and other goods. If they tried to attack too near the coast of France the watchers in the towers would give the alarm, and then boats and men would be sent out to fight the pirate boats.

There were smugglers also. The men in the towers kept a particularly sharp watch for these. The object of the smuggler was to avoid paying any of the Customs dues that the Celys had to pay at Calais, just as they had already paid in London. So the smugglers bought wool and then put it on boats hidden away at some small town on the south coast of England. One dark night they would set off to cross the Channel, hoping to land the wool in some small harbour in France. They would probably try to get to some place quite close to Calais. Then they could hope to do a deal with one of the merchants who came there. Sometimes the smugglers were caught and punished, but they often succeeded in smuggling wool, as well as other goods.

Now we can see why it was very necessary to have the watchmen in the towers, to keep a sharp lookout for both pirates and smugglers. We can be sure that they would have a good look at the ship on which the Cely wool was stowed. But that boat was on lawful business, so they would not stop her. Thus the voyage ended, at the quays of Calais.

41

AT CALAIS

On the quay George Cely would be standing watching as the boat slowly made her way alongside and tied up. A letter from London sent by an earlier boat had told him to expect the wool. William Cely had written to him:

> My master has shipped his fells at the Port of London, which fells you must receive and pay the *freight*.

This letter would have been brought to George in his lodgings in one of the houses that lined the narrow streets. He did not have a house of his own. Probably lodgings were more convenient as he was not married and had much business to attend to. After getting the letter George Cely would have gone several times to the harbour to make enquiries whether the ship had yet been sighted. When he heard that it had been sighted he would go on to the quay to wait for it. He would want to be the first to jump on board to greet the master of the ship, and to enquire about the wool they were bringing him. He knew just where the wool was stowed on the ship and how it was packed. When William Cely had written to tell him it was coming he had also told him where to look for it when he got on the boat. He wrote in the letter how many sarplers there were, and then went on to tell that there were

> five lying near the mast, one before the mast, others underneath.

We must expect that George Cely was very eager to see what wool had been sent and how good it was. His business was to sell it well and send a good account of the sale to his father in London. But before he could sell it there was much to be done.

First of all, before George was even allowed to take the sarplers off the boat, he had to pay the Master the charge for carrying them. When this was settled, the men George had brought with him picked up the sarplers and carried them off the ship. Then there was more money to be paid out before they could be taken away from the quay. This was called primage or port dues.

George Cely had to keep a careful account of what he paid out. Here is an entry from one of the account books:

> item. the 4th day of August. Paid by me in the name of my father Richard Cely unto James Holland, master in the BLYTHE of London the freight of 2 sarplers (each) 6s. 8d. Primage (that is port dues) 13s. 6d.

When this money had been paid, the sarplers had to be taken to the warehouse where officers of the Staple waited for it. We remember how at the London Customs House the wool had been weighed, seals had been placed on the sarplers to show this had been done, and cockets had been written out. Now in Calais the wool was weighed again, and the weights were compared with what had been written down on the cocket in London. Sometimes it weighed more. Then the merchants would be accused of trying to smuggle in the extra without paying for it. But the merchants said this was unfair. They said they had not been able to touch the sarplers since they had been weighed in London and put on board. They said it was much more likely that the wool had got wet with rain or from the sea breaking over the ship. If the wool were wet of course it would weigh more.

A street scene such as George Cely would see in Calais.

A still more anxious moment was when a sarpler was opened to look at the quality of the wool. Generally the officials would pick one sarpler at random out of all those belonging to one merchant. This is what happened one day to the Cely sarplers. They were lying in the warehouse waiting to be passed. William Cely was in charge. The official of the Staple came in and asked for one particular sarpler to be opened. He found it was not good wool, as it ought to be, but only very 'middling'. But William Cely asked for another sarpler to be opened. That was full of good wool and was marked accordingly. Then William had the middling wool put in that packet also, so it looked as if it were all good. This sounds like cheating, and it was cheating. There was a great deal of this kind of artfulness. We can see how necessary it was to have all the wool carefully examined. For if the wool were not good the merchants who came to buy it would soon complain, and that would be bad for English trade.

The merchants who came to look at the wool and buy it if they were pleased with it, came mostly from Flanders, particularly the towns of Bruges and Ghent. We can imagine them riding along the roads on the rather heavy-looking horses for which Flanders was celebrated. But the heavy-looking horses were very sturdy and they carried their masters, sometimes rather stout people, very well. The Flemish merchants would not look much different from the English merchants. They wore the same long cloth dresses belted at the waist. They had the same kind of shoes made of leather or cloth. They wore flat hats, and each had a heavy cloak to fling over himself and his horse if it were raining. It might very well be raining, for Flanders can be a very wet place indeed, with muddy roads.

When they reached Calais the Flemish merchants rode

along the cobbled streets to the Guildhall, where the English merchants waited for them. Here you can see this fine building:

George Cely was there. He probably knew some of the foreign merchants already, for he would have done business with them before. Now he would wave a greeting to those he knew, hoping they would come straight over to where he had his sacks of wool all ready for inspection. Once again the wool was pulled out and held up to the light and well rubbed between the fingers of the buyers. They wanted to be sure it was the best wool for their purpose. And of course there was always the risk that some less good wool had got into the sack or been put there or perhaps had got some other things mixed in with it. That is why the washing and picking over had been done so carefully in the Cotswolds and then the wool looked through again in London.

When the merchants were at last satisfied with the quality of the wool, they offered George Cely a price. Then would come the bargaining. George wanted to get as much as he could: he had to satisfy his father away in London. The buyer would want to give as little as he could. At last they would come to an agreement. The money was sometimes handed straight over. Sometimes instead the foreign merchants would give George a note about the money owing to him. For the note George could either get money in Calais or else send it to his father in England, who would draw the money there by arrangement with the foreign merchants.

Here is a merchant counting out his money:

When the deal was made it is to be hoped everybody was pleased. The Flemish merchants were glad to get the good English wool. And George would be very glad to be able to write to his father that he had sold it to them at a good price.

47

After this there would very likely be a merry dinner. The Flemish merchants and the English merchants would eat and drink together, and we may be sure they would tell each other many tales. Sometimes a merchant would have had an adventure on his way to Calais. Perhaps an English merchant would tell how his ship was chased by pirates in the English Channel. Or a Flemish merchant would say how some highwaymen had tried to steal his money from him as he rode along the Flemish roads. We can be sure too that each would tell the other how clever he had been on certain occasions at buying the wool at a good price if he were a Flemish merchant or at selling it at a good price if he were an Englishman.

At last the foreign merchants would ride away again to their own towns. The sacks of wool would be put on the backs of horses or mules just as they had been for their transport from the Cotswolds to London. When the merchants and the wool reached Ghent or Bruges or any of the other towns where the weavers lived, the sacks were taken to the place of weaving and opened. We can be sure that the merchants who had stayed at home and not travelled to Calais also wanted to inspect the wool and test it. If it were not the kind of wool they hoped for, those who bought the wool would hear about it. But the buyers were always very well trained in how to examine wool, so they usually bought very carefully. At last the wool would go to the weavers, who set it on their looms to be woven into the cloth for which Flanders was famous.

It is likely that when George Cely had made a good sale in Calais he would go back to England in one of the little ships for a short stay in the family house at Mark Lane.

Then he would tell his father and brothers tales of Calais and of the foreign merchants he had met. Of course they would be chiefly interested to hear of the selling of the wool and the people who had bought it. But he might tell them too of some of his own adventures.

For instance, there was the day when he rode with friends along the road by the sea to Boulogne. You can see from a map that Boulogne was not very far from Calais. As they passed out of the gate at Calais they had seen something very grim. This was the gallows on which criminals were hung. But there was nothing grim about the trip of George and his friends to Boulogne. They went there to enjoy themselves. They had a good dinner at which they drank wine. During the dinner a minstrel came and played to them. We do not know what instrument he played, but very likely it was a lute or a pipe, like one of these:

After the dinner they did not go straight back to Calais but remained at Boulogne for the night. Here is the bill for all they did:

For the dinner	5s. 3d.
For the wine at that dinner	4s.
As we lay all night, wine, bed and horse	4s. 10d.
Gave the minstrel	4s.

But when they came back to Calais they did not ride on horseback from Boulogne. Perhaps they were too tired after their merry dinner the night before. Whatever the reason, they hired a cart in which to return. It cost them 9s.—which seems a great deal compared with what the dinner cost.

Other merry occasions about which George might have told his relations were shooting matches with bows and arrows. This was a favourite sport. There was a stretch of green grass quite near one of the quays in Boulogne where such shooting matches were held. It was called Paradise. At one of these matches the married English merchants challenged the bachelors. There were twelve married men on one side and twelve bachelors on the other. They were to shoot at a range of 200 yards. The losers were to pay for a dinner for all the twenty-four. The dinner was to cost 12d. a head. Unfortunately we do not know which side won the match, though you can see one man is keeping the score very carefully.

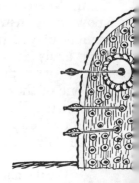

Although George would have all these things to tell his family on his visit home, we get an impression that sometimes he wished he lived in the house in Mark Lane all the time instead of having to go back to Calais. In particular he missed very much his horses, his dogs, and his hawks. He was a sportsman and he was very fond of all of them. Of course, he kept some in Calais. After one of his visits to England he took quite a number of grey-hounds back to Calais with him. Another time a horse would be sent out to him. Imagine how difficult this would be in a little boat. But it was often done. The horse would be made to walk on to the boat from the seashore. It may well have been very frightened. We can be sure that it was very glad to find itself walking again on to the firm land when the boat put into the harbour at Calais. We can also be sure that its master was very pleased indeed to go down to the quay to meet it and lead it back to his lodgings. Perhaps George Cely was even more pleased to see the horse than he was to see the wool.

Even hawks would be sent out sometimes. One reason for this was that hawks were very dear to buy in Calais. They were so dear that no ordinary merchant could afford to buy them, only noblemen. This is what George wrote:

> Here hath come several hawks but they be so dear that no man buyeth them but my lord.

So George was not entirely without his dogs, his horses, and his hawks, even in Calais. But there were others he had left behind in England which could not be sent out to him. He was very fond of them and was always asking how they were getting on and what had happened to them. Very often he got good news. His servant wrote from England:

> Sir, Bayard your horse does well and so does your other horse too.

Another letter, this time from his brother Richard, told him that:

Your black horse and your grey in London are well.

George must have been pleased to get this good news, but there was another occasion when he had the sad information that one of his dogs was dead. The poor thing had had fourteen puppies and then had died. Ten of the poor little puppies had died too. But George was told that the other four were alive and were being very well taken care of.

The family in Mark Lane found it useful to have George in Calais for other reasons besides the selling of the wool. There were goods made in France which the English liked to buy. When George went home he would be told to get these and send them over to England. Or a letter would be sent to him telling him to do so.

One of the things he was told to buy was *linen*. This was probably linen woven in one of the Flemish towns. The Flemish linen, like Flemish woollen cloth, was excellent and very much sought after. On one occasion George was told to buy "five *ells* of fine linen for sheets". On another his mother asked him to get her some *calico*. She did not say for what she wanted it. Perhaps it was for a gown. At any rate George wrote and told her that he had got it and would send it out "by the next ship that goes to London". He was often asked too to send gloves. Gloves had been made in England for many years before the days of the Celys, but the French and Flemish glove-makers were celebrated. The gloves they made were thought to be much better than any to be got in England. So the Cely family made use of George to buy gloves and send them back to London. Once he bought a number of pairs in the Flemish town of Louvain. Another time his brother Richard reminded him that he had asked him to buy

half a dozen pair of French gloves, three for men and three for women.

We suspect that when those gloves reached England Richard's mother and brothers wore them very proudly. Probably they were much admired. The women's gloves sometimes had embroidery on them.

So George, who had to live in Calais, was very useful to his family. But of course it was the selling of the wool that mattered. It is like the story of the house that Jack built. First the sheep-farmers and their shepherds far away in the Cotswolds had to rear their sheep. Then when wool was good and thick on the sheep's backs it was cut off. Next one of the Celys rode down from London to look at the wool and buy it for his father. When it got to London it was put on the boats. It crossed the Channel to Calais. At Calais it was sold by George Cely, who was waiting for it, to the Flemish merchants. They took it away to Ghent and other cities to their weavers to turn into cloth.

The sheep-farmers were paid for their wool. The captains of the boats were paid for taking it to Calais. The Flemish merchants paid George Cely for it.

"It was the sheep that paid for all."

THERE were some people who disapproved of the Celys because they shipped so much wool to Calais. These were the cloth-manufacturers. For centuries the English had been weaving cloth, and by the time of the Celys they could produce not only rough stuffs for poor folks, but fine materials for lords and kings.

Many hands were needed in cloth-making, for there were many things to do before the tangled, greasy, dirty fleece off the sheep's back was transformed into a fine, smooth piece of cloth.

SORTING, SCOURING, PICKING. The long wool had to be sorted from the short and then each graded into different qualities. Then the wool was thoroughly scoured in a stream and beaten with sticks. The last bits of dirt and bad wool were picked out by hand.

CARDING AND COMBING disentangled the fibres of wool and got them all lying one way. Short wool was done on two 'cards' like hair-brushes with wire bristles. The wool was placed on one card and brushed with the other. Long wool was combed out with combs that had long, pointed iron teeth. At the end the wool was

in a fleecy roll.

SPINNING drew out the wool into one long, fine, tightly-twisted thread. This was usually done with a distaff—a stick with a forked top—and a spindle, which was a fairly heavy spinning top. You stuck the roll of wool into the forked top and tied an end to the spindle. Then with your right hand you pulled out and twisted the wool, while the spindle, dangling down, also kept pulling out and twisting it into one long thread which could then be wound on a reel. Sometimes a spinning-wheel was used instead. These three jobs were nearly always done by women, and in the picture on page 54 you can see them at work.

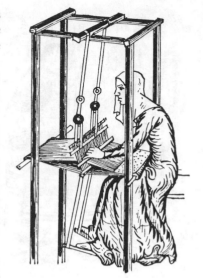

WEAVING THE CLOTH. This was usually a man's job. It was done on a loom not so very different from the ones used today, except that it was smaller and worked by hand instead of power. If you do not know already, find out how cloth is woven today on a power-loom. Then compare it with this picture of a hand-loom:

FULLING. Now the 'raw cloth' had to be cleaned and thickened. This was done with white stuff called fuller's earth, a kind of washing-powder which could be dug out of the earth in certain places. You soaked the cloth in water with the fuller's earth and beat it hard. This could be done by men trampling the cloth with their bare feet. But clever people had invented a water-mill which turned in a stream and beat the cloth as it turned. So many cloth-makers used fulling-mills.

STRETCHING. Next the cloth was dried and stretched to its proper length and width on frames called tenters, to which it was fastened by—have you guessed?—tenter-hooks! Often special open spaces in town were kept as tenter-grounds.

ROWING. Now the cloth was brushed up by a rower. He used teasels, the prickly heads of a plant which grows in many parts of England. They look like thistles and make just the right kind of brush for this job.

SHEARING. Then the shearman cut the surface of the cloth to a smooth, even finish with a great pair of scissors.

DRAWING. Last of all, the drawer mended any bad patches in the cloth.

But what about dyeing the cloth the gorgeous colours that men as well as women loved in the fifteenth century? Dyeing could be done either before the wool was woven into cloth or after. Here are some dyers at work with their great vat full of dye:

The dyes came from many places. Three common ones— woad (blue), weld (yellow), madder (red)—were made from plants grown in this country, though often imported as well. Saffron, a bright yellow made from crocuses, was usually imported and the rarer dyes always had to be brought in ships; for instance, vermilion, from a mineral by the Red Sea, brasil red, from an Indian tree, and—most precious of all—the brilliant scarlet, made from a tiny insect found in the Mediterranean.

In all these different processes there were many chances to cheat. The sorter could mix in bad wool with good and pretend it was all good. The dyer could use poor dyes. The weaver might weave carefully at the ends of the rolls, which were easily seen, but carelessly in the middle. When hanging the wet cloths out on the tenter-frames it was a great temptation to stretch them too much. Finally, the drawer might cover up the holes and bad patches in a way that deceived the buyer. The town councils were always making rules to stop such cheating, for they wanted good cloth made, so that many buyers would come. Bad work and cheating drove the buyers away.

Different places in England specialized in varieties of cloth which were often named after them. You can easily find out where Lincoln Green, Stamford Scarlet and Beverley Blue were made. Worsted and Kersey were two kinds of cloth named after two villages, one in Norfolk and the other in Suffolk.

At first most of the best cloth was made in Yorkshire and East Anglia, but by the time of the Celys the West of England was becoming famous for its fine 'broadcloths'. South and west of the Cotswolds (where the sheep grazed), all along the river valleys, spinners, dyers, weavers, fullers and the rest were hard at work. At Castle Combe there were seventy weavers, fullers and dyers living down by the river. Along the Stroud valley, the Avon valley, the Wylie valley, the cloth-workers gathered and the cloth trade hummed. Why did they choose to work by the rivers? You should know the answer to that question now. Sometimes they worked at home; sometimes a big clothier gathered them together in one workshop. One of these was Thomas Blanket of Bristol; you can guess how he got his name.

Altogether, a great many people in England took part in making cloth which they sold, not only in all the markets of England, but in Flanders, Italy and other parts of Europe. English cloth, like English wool, sold well.

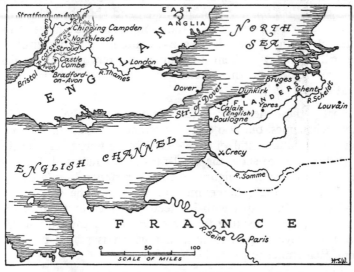

Map showing places connected with the wool trade.

57

HOW WE KNOW

The Celys, as you know, wrote letters to each other. They had to write about the wool business, but they also tell us in their letters about their lives—what they were doing, whom they met, and things they wanted. We still have these letters, as well as others written by various merchants and travellers in the fifteenth century. Altogether, they give us a wonderful picture of the lives of these fifteenth-century men.

Two other sources from which we learn a great deal are:

(1) *Pictures which fifteenth-century people drew:* of sheep and shepherds, of horses and ships, of London and Calais, and of many other things they saw. All the pictures in this book are made from drawings done by the people who actually saw these things.

(2) *Buildings which fifteenth-century people built:* houses for themselves, like the one in Mark Lane, and churches which they either built or enlarged. With the money made from wool, they were able to make these houses and churches very beautiful. We can still see many of them standing in different parts of England and can remember the wool-merchants who worked hard to build them.

Finally, these men liked to leave after them on their tombs, not only their names, but also their appearance. So in many churches there are 'monumental brasses'—flat, brass figures on the floor or wall, carved to show the wool-merchant's face and clothes as well as his name. The figure on page 6 is drawn from a brass in Northleach Church. Sometimes, to show that he was a wool-merchant, he is drawn with his feet on a sack of wool or on a sheep. If you are looking for these brasses on the church floor, you often have to pull aside a mat which is placed to protect them. Remember to put it back again.

THINGS TO DO

1. Paint a picture of the Cely family at home in the great parlour.

2. Write a conversation about sheep-farming between the two shepherds in the picture on page 12.

3. Read in class the scene of the sheep-shearing feast in Shakespeare's ' Winter's Tale '.

4. Write a letter from the young lady to William Midwinter (see page 21) telling him what she thinks of Richard Cely.

5. Draw a picture of the MARGARET CELY sailing into Calais harbour.

6. Write a short story or play about smuggling wool from England to France.

7. Write a letter from George Cely in Calais telling his father in London all the news.

8. Write an essay or draw a series of pictures describing all the stages between the wool on the sheep's back and the cloth made in Flanders.

9. Find out if your part of England has ever been famous for sheep.   If so, try to discover:

(a) if there have been or are still any cloth-mills;
(b) if there have been famous wool-merchants or clothiers whose names are still known;
(c) if their houses are still standing;
(d) if their tombs or gravestones can still be seen;
(e) if they built or enlarged any churches, or built almshouses or left money for the poor, etc.

10. If you can visit a wool-merchants' or clothiers' church, find out if there are any monumental brasses of them.   If you can get someone to show you the method, you could make "brass-rubbings" of these figures and decorate your classroom with them.

GLOSSARY

bushel: measure for dry goods (wheat, fruit, etc.) equal to 8 gallons.

calico: coarse cotton cloth.

canvas: coarse cloth made from hemp, used for tents, sails, etc.

cobbled: paved with small, round stones.

cocket: paper on which the weight of the wool was written.

crook: stick with curved top used by shepherds.

ell: measure for cloth, equal to $1\frac{1}{4}$ yards.

ewe: mother sheep.

falconer: man who looks after birds called falcons or hawks.

fell: skin of sheep.

fleece: coat of wool cut off the sheep.

Flemish: belonging to the country of Flanders.

freight: charge to be paid for goods carried.

friar: member of a religious order.

heron: large bird with long legs living in watery places.

kinswoman: relation.

linen: fine cloth made from flax.

Lord Chancellor: the chief judge.

matins: morning service.

nosegay: bunch of flowers.

pack-horse: horse to carry packs or bundles of goods.

pasture: grassy land where sheep, etc., feed.

peck: measure equal to 2 gallons.

pipe: musical instrument made from a hollow reed or stick.

pottle: small pot.

quartern: quarter (28 lb.).

resin: used to rub on bow-strings.

sarpler: big bundle of wool done up in canvas.

to shear: to cut off.

staple: special town to which all wool to be sold must be sent.

strand: shore.

stuff: stout cloth.

substance: riches.

victualled: provided with food.